HOW TO START A FOOD TRUCK

All the Crap Nobody Told Me

K. L. ANDERSON

May God bless this content and the reader!

To My Incredible Husband,

You are the muscle that powers our food truck dreams and the unwavering support that propels our success. Your tireless efforts and endless support allow me to explore creativity without bounds. Together, we make an unstoppable team. This guide is a testament to our partnership and shared journey.

With love and gratitude,

Kesha

Contents

Introduction

You've likely spotted those random hot dog or taco trucks and thought, "Hey, I could do that on the weekends and make some money." Well, here's a reality check – running a food truck business is no walk in the park. It's hard work, and there's more to it than meets the eye.

Whether you're eyeing one food truck or considering a fleet, approaching this journey and investment requires a serious business mindset. This venture demands genuine commitment. If you purchased this book, it's likely because you're genuinely seeking valuable insights, contemplating a real move forward, or simply curious about the nitty-gritty of starting out. In any case, I'm thrilled you're here.

Now, if your idea is to grab any random truck and sell just about anything, then by all means, go for it. But I'll be upfront – this book might not be the right fit for you, and honestly, the whole venture may not be right for you.

Here's the deal: before you even think about making that first sale, you need to build out your shell and set up your files and trackers. In other words, get organized from the get-go. Starting with a sense of order is crucial to staying in control. Knowing the cost of each menu item is paramount – don't just buy supplies and sell products without understanding if you're turning a profit.

I'll guide you through this process, but I won't be using fancy accounting methods. Just good old-fashioned Excel spreadsheets, maybe a bit of counting on fingers and toes. If that sounds uncomfortable to you, once again, this might not be the course for you. But if you're up for a practical, hands-on approach to getting your food truck business off the ground, then you're in the right place.

Let's dive in together.

About The Author

Allow me to provide you with some insights into my background. Following a distinguished 21-year career as a retired Army Officer, I transitioned into entrepreneurship with a clear vision of owning and operating my own business post-military service. Embracing a diverse range of interests, I ventured into the business world with the confidence to explore various opportunities.

Over the course of more than two decades, my professional journey has encompassed roles in inventory management, customer service, asset accountability, organizational leadership, and process improvement. My academic credentials include a management/logistics degree from Park University, a business and management degree from Excelsior College, and a master's degree

in transportation and logistics management from AMU. Additionally, I have enriched my entrepreneurial knowledge through certificate-level courses from Cornell University.

One notable aspect of my expertise lies in successfully owning and operating a thriving food truck and restaurant named Road-Tisserie. This practical experience adds a unique dimension to my professional profile. It's important to emphasize that my journey is a collaborative effort, with my dedicated husband, also a retired Army veteran and a qualified chef with a degree in hospitality management, actively contributing to the operation of our food truck and restaurant. Together, we bring a wealth of skills and experiences to our entrepreneurial endeavors.

Introduction To the Journey

Whether you're here out of curiosity or serious interest, I'm thrilled you've made it this far. Starting a food truck is not a whimsical endeavor; it's a business, and we'll treat it as such. In this guide, I aim to provide you with genuine insights and practical advice, steering away from overly technical jargon. So, if you're ready for a down-to-earth conversation about starting your food truck, let's hit the road!

Throughout this journey, I'll walk you through each agency you need to visit and demystify the process. I'll share some valuable insights, including things I wish I had known but had to figure out from scratch. To make your life easier, I'll provide links to templates that you can personalize and make your own. So, buckle up for a comprehensive and insightful ride into the world of food truck entrepreneurship!

About This Book

In the realm of diving into the food truck business, you'll find tons of resources out there, all dishing out useful tips. But let me tell you, having walked the path of entrepreneurship in the food truck world myself, I noticed a big gap that this book is set to fill. We're not just going to skim through the usual stuff about permits and regulations; we're diving deep into the nitty-gritty details that often get brushed aside in the hustle. Get ready for insights that go beyond the norm!

This guide is your go-to resource for real, practical answers to the multitude of challenges that come with being a hopeful food truck owner. It's not just about theories; it dives into the hands-on aspects, tackling everything from landing gigs to the ins and outs of getting your hands on essential supplies. It's more than a rulebook – it's a collection of my personal stories and the lessons I gained from the ups and downs of launching and running a thriving food truck.

As we take this journey together, we're not fixated solely on the legal stuff. We're getting into the nitty-gritty details that truly matter in the day-to-day grind of running a food truck business. Whether you're figuring out how to snag opportunities, searching for quality ingredients, or unraveling the mysteries of pricing and crafting a menu, consider this book your practical companion.

Consider this book a candid conversation over a kitchen table, where practical advice is shared, and the nuances of the food truck business are explored with a down-to-earth perspective. It's not just about starting a business; it's about successfully maneuvering through the challenges that come with it.

ICONS OFFER A SIDE NOTE

 Fees Are Likely to Apply

 Downloadable Template Available

 Suggests a Trick or Technique

 Caution or Warning

 Tie it Together

CHAPTER 1
Steps To Getting Started

Now, let's get into the meaty part of the guide – the steps to kickstarting your food truck business. Rather than presenting you with a checklist upfront, I'll share the practical steps I took.

Commercial Kitchen/Commissary

Let's set the stage for culinary excellence! When you don't have the luxury of your home kitchen being certified as a commercial kitchen, a local kitchen becomes the backbone of your food truck operation – it's not just any kitchen; it's your culinary headquarters, where your delightful creations come to life.

So, why a commissary? It's more than just a kitchen; it's a hub of essential services. Imagine a space where you can prep and store your menu items effortlessly. No more hassles about where to dispose of waste – your commissary takes care of grey water, trash, and grease disposal.

In the intricate dance of the food truck world, a reliable commissary becomes your partner in equipment maintenance. Keep the heart of your operation – your food truck – in top-notch condition with the convenience of regular maintenance services provided by your trusted commissary.

Remember, it's not just about the kitchen; it's about having a culinary sanctuary that offers a suite of services, ensuring your food truck journey is not only delectable but also seamlessly supported behind the scenes. Welcome to the heart of your culinary operations – your commercial kitchen and commissary.

Even if your food truck is equipped with everything a full commercial kitchen offers, it's a legal requirement to have a separate commercial kitchen or commissary.

In smaller towns, finding available commercial kitchen space for rent can be a challenge, leading to fewer food trucks in those areas. However, in larger cities, the demand is higher, prompting the creation of commercial spaces to accommodate numerous food trucks. While not every food truck owner may strictly adhere to regulations, I strongly advise against taking such risks. It's crucial to stay within the bounds of the law. The last thing you want is someone falling ill and facing an investigation. Always prioritize compliance for the safety of your customers and the success of your food truck business.

This particular aspect often becomes a stumbling block for many aspiring food truck entrepreneurs, preventing them from fully diving into the game. However, if you're blessed to have access to kitchen space, let's proceed!

Health Department

Now that you've successfully secured your commercial kitchen and have the lease in hand, it's time to prepare for the health inspection. Make sure to also obtain a copy of the kitchen owner's health department permit for your records, adding an extra layer of documentation to your preparations.

Before you roll up your sleeves to build or buy your food truck, make a friendly call to your local Health Department. Each state has its own rules, so it's like getting the insider scoop. They'll spill the beans on what your food truck needs to pass inspection – a kind of health check for your truck.

Usually, the health department will give you a checklist in the form of an information packet, and you'll have to fill it out and send it back. Completing the packet might involve more than just basic details. For instance, let's say you bought a food trailer online, and it only has a handwashing sink as its sole water source. According to the checklist, you might be required to have a three-compartment sink. In that case, you'll need to install one before scheduling your appointment with the health department. Additionally, you may need a fire suppression system, and without a doubt, you'll need fire extinguishers, which leads us to our next part.

Fire Extinguishers And Suppression System

This isn't handled by the fire department or the Fire Marshall. You will need them inspected and tagged. You'll have to reach out to a local professional and cover the cost of this service. Remember, it's an annual requirement, and yes, there's a fee involved. After getting this done, get in touch with the Fire Marshall to arrange the inspection.

Fire Marshall Inspection

Now, onto the main event – the Fire Marshall inspection. This isn't just a formality; it's a crucial checkpoint for the safety of your operation. Reach out to the local Fire Marshall to schedule a thorough inspection of your food truck.

Local requirements might throw in a curveball or two, so make sure you're up to date with what's expected. The Fire Marshall will scrutinize various aspects, including your fire extinguishers and hood system. It's a comprehensive safety dance to ensure your mobile kitchen complies and is ready to roll safely into the food truck scene.

Ensure you've got the local health department's checklist in your hands. Once you've acquired that, you've secured a commercial kitchen—whether rented or self-built—with the necessary inspection permit. Your food truck has undergone inspection, but before reaching out to the health department, it's crucial to have a local professional inspect and tag your fire extinguishers and fire suppression system. Once that's done, the Fire Marshal steps in for their inspection, providing the essential paperwork indicating your compliance. With all these elements aligned, you're ready to schedule the health department's inspection for your food truck or trailer. Initiate the process with your local county health department for a smooth journey ahead.

Insurance

Protect your dream on wheels! Securing insurance for your food truck is a crucial step in safeguarding your business against unforeseen bumps in the road. Choose an insurance provider well-versed in the unique needs of food trucks to ensure comprehensive coverage.

Cover your bases – both literally and figuratively. Your insurance should extend its protective embrace over not just your food truck but also the trusty vehicle hauling it.

Accidents happen, breakdowns occur – that's where roadside assistance comes to the rescue. Consider adding this invaluable service to your insurance plan, providing you with a safety net on the open road.

Remember, it's not just about preparing for the unexpected; it's about having the confidence that, come what may, your food truck venture is shielded by a robust insurance plan. So, buckle up and drive with peace of mind that your business is covered against life's unpredictable twists and turns.

Registration

Now that your food truck is all set to hit the road, it's time to make it official with the Department of Motor Vehicles (DMV). Think of it as giving your truck its passport to the streets.

So, grab their checklist of requirements or make a phone call so you will know what to bring with you. Once you've nailed the checklist and paid the piper, your food truck is ready to roll with its official road credentials. It's not just a truck anymore; it's a DMV-approved street sensation. Get ready to take your culinary journey to the streets!

Now, we've got our investment covered with a solid insurance plan, and we've officially registered our truck or trailer with the Department of Motor Vehicles, snagging our registration and temporary plates.

State Tax License

Next up, let's get that sales tax license sorted for your state. I handled this step online, precisely during the build and before the health inspection. Just hit the internet and search for the Department of Revenue along with your state name, or you can specifically look for "How to Apply for a (your state) sales tax license." They'll usually mail it to you and don't forget to set up your online account for filing returns.

Once you've hit submit on your application, it's time to set up camp in the online world. Create your online account, and this isn't just about making a profile – it's your hub for filing returns. Imagine it as the control center for keeping the taxman happy and your food truck finances in check.

Why is this step crucial? Well, it's the secret sauce to staying on the right side of tax regulations. It's not just paperwork; it's your shield against tax-related headaches. So, dive into the online realm, get that state sales tax license, and let the compliance adventure begin!

City Tax License

Once you've secured your state tax license, the next step is to go for your city tax license. During this process, they usually ask for a copy of your state tax license. I handled the city tax application locally, although, in your state, you might have the option to do it online. Don't forget to set up your online account for filing returns – it's a convenient way to keep everything organized. Note: The city tax filing will probably be included in the account you created for the state BUT you had better make sure. You want to ensure everyone gets their money.

Now that we've completed the city and sales tax ID registration, we've also gone ahead and set up our online accounts for seamless tax filing. Depending on your sales volume, you'll probably fall into the monthly filing category. It's essential to stay on top of these obligations to ensure smooth financial operations for your food truck business.

City Hall

Now, let's make it official with your local City Hall. Reach out to them to secure that golden ticket – your mobile food vendor license. It's the key that unlocks the doors to the city streets for your food truck.

Alright, so here's the deal – the licensing game for food trucks can be a bit of a maze, and it varies from one place to another. In many cases, you might need a separate license for each city where you're planning to roll out your food truck. It's a city-by-city thing, you know? Some areas might have a joint or county-wide license that covers a bunch of cities but don't bank on it. You've got to dive into the local regulations and make sure you're covered in every city you plan to operate. Check with the local government folks and licensing agencies –

they'll have the lowdown on what you need for each stop on your food truck journey.

Files And Tracking

Now, before we delve into other areas like locations and supplies, let's talk about something crucial – building your files. These are not your typical balance sheets; these are the practical files that nobody told me about. Embark on the organized path to success by establishing a comprehensive system of files and trackers. Think of them as your trusty sidekicks in this culinary adventure, keeping you on track and ahead of the game. Here's a sneak peek into the essential files and trackers that might just become your business best friends:

Inventory Log

Maintenance Schedule

Event Calendar

Licensing and Permits

Financial Tracker

Supplier Contacts

Menu Performance Tracker

Event Details

Tax Wisdom

Receipts and More

10 AREAS

Create Hard Copy and Digital Files

Digital Resources Included

CHAPTER 2
Inventory Log

Starting with the inventory log is crucial, especially for those new to the world of food service. I find it a bit challenging to explain, particularly to beginners. If you're already experienced with inventory, you might have a different and perhaps more effective approach. But personally, this is how my mind keeps track. I'll do my best to stay on course and focus on the topic at hand.

An Inventory Log: A Blueprint for Culinary Success

In the bustling world of food trucks, where every dish is a masterpiece in motion, the importance of an Inventory Log cannot be overstated. Keep a meticulous record of all your supplies, ensuring you never run out of key ingredients. An organized inventory log is your compass in navigating the ebb and flow of your stock.

Defining the Inventory Log: An Inventory Log is a meticulously maintained record of all the supplies, ingredients, and goods stocked in your food truck. It serves as a real-time snapshot of what you have on hand, from fresh produce to spices, ensuring you're well-equipped to create your culinary delights.

Key Components of an Inventory Log:

1. **Item Details:**
   - Catalog every item in your inventory, from the basics to the specialty ingredients that give your dishes that unique flair. Include details like name, quantity, and unit measurements.

- Your list might require listing an item twice because you could acquire the item from different vendors at different times. It's important to keep track of the cost per vendor, the packaging details, and the quantity in each package. For instance, if you usually order 12" tortilla shells from U.S. Foods, and a case with six packs of 12 costs $40.39, but due to a busy week, you need to buy them from Costco, where a pack of twenty 10" tortilla shells costs $7.92. If you'll be using both vendors frequently in this manner, it's necessary to track them on the same inventory log.

2. **Reorder Points:**

- Set thresholds for each item, indicating the minimum quantity at which you should reorder. This proactive approach helps prevent stockouts and ensures you're always ready for service.

3. **Expiration Dates:**

- Especially crucial for perishable items, noting expiration dates ensures you use ingredients at their freshest. Minimizing waste and delivering top-notch quality to your customers become natural byproducts.

How an Inventory Log Can Help:

1. **Optimal Stock Management:**

- Avoid the chaos of running out of essential ingredients during a busy service. An Inventory Log provides a clear overview of stock levels, enabling you to make informed decisions about when to restock.

2. **Cost Control:**

- Track the cost of ingredients and monitor fluctuations. This information empowers you to identify cost-saving opportunities, negotiate better deals with suppliers, and ultimately enhance your profit margins.

- Effective cost control management plays a crucial role in efficient menu planning. While understanding the overall cost of ingredients is essential, delving into the specifics, such as the cost of each slice of cheese or each tablespoon of mayonnaise, is equally important.

3. **Efficient Menu Planning:**

    ▪ Plan your menu with precision. Analyze which dishes are more resource-intensive and adjust your offerings accordingly. The Inventory Log acts as a strategic tool in shaping a menu that balances culinary excellence with operational efficiency.

    ▪ Craft your menu with precision. Evaluate the resource intensity of each dish and adjust accordingly. The Inventory Log serves as a strategic tool, guiding the creation of a menu that strikes a balance between culinary excellence and operational efficiency.

4. **Minimizing Food Waste:**

    ▪ By understanding your inventory flow, you can minimize wastage. The Inventory Log helps you manage quantities effectively, reducing the likelihood of unused items reaching their expiration dates.

5. **Streamlined Ordering Process:**

    ▪ Simplify the reordering process by having a clear overview of what needs replenishing. This efficiency not only saves time but ensures you have what you need when you need it.

Inventory Log.xlsx

CHAPTER 3
Maintenance Schedule

A well-maintained food truck is a happy food truck. Create a schedule for regular check-ups, repairs, and maintenance. This ensures your wheels keep turning smoothly, both metaphorically and literally.

A Maintenance Schedule: Nurturing Your Food Truck for Longevity

Just like a finely tuned instrument, your food truck requires regular care and attention to ensure it operates at its peak performance. Enter the Maintenance Schedule – your roadmap to keeping every component humming smoothly. Let's delve into what a Maintenance Schedule is and how this vital tool can be the guardian angel of your culinary chariot.

Defining the Maintenance Schedule: A Maintenance Schedule is a pre-planned timetable outlining routine checks, repairs, and preventive maintenance tasks for all aspects of your food truck. From the engine's purr to the cleanliness of your kitchen equipment, this schedule is your proactive strategy for averting breakdowns and extending the lifespan of your mobile kitchen.

Key Components of a Maintenance Schedule:

1. **Engine and Vehicle Components:**
   - Regular oil changes, filter replacements, and checks on belts and hoses keep your food truck's engine running smoothly, ensuring reliability on the road.

2. **Kitchen Equipment:**

   ▪ Scheduled inspections and cleaning routines for cooking appliances, refrigeration units, and other kitchen essentials prevent unexpected malfunctions during service hours.

3. **Tires and Brakes:**

   ▪ Periodic inspections of tire conditions and brake systems are crucial for the safety of your staff and customers. A well-maintained braking system and reliable tires are non-negotiables.

4. **Generator and Power Supply:**

   ▪ If your food truck relies on a generator, regular maintenance ensures a consistent power supply. This includes checking fuel levels, changing filters, and inspecting electrical connections.

5. **Propane Systems:**

   ▪ For trucks equipped with propane for cooking, a thorough check of the propane system is necessary to prevent leaks and ensure safe operations.

How a Maintenance Schedule Can Help:

1. **Preventing Costly Breakdowns:**

   ▪ By addressing potential issues before they escalate, a Maintenance Schedule helps you avoid sudden breakdowns that could lead to expensive repairs and downtime.

2. **Ensuring Food Safety:**

   ▪ Regular checks on kitchen equipment guarantee that your food is prepared in a safe and hygienic environment, safeguarding the well-being of your customers.

3. **Extending Equipment Lifespan:**

   - Routine maintenance prolongs the life of your food truck and kitchen equipment, protecting your investment and reducing the need for premature replacements.

4. **Enhancing Reliability:**

   - A well-maintained food truck is a reliable one. Whether you're navigating city streets or serving at events, knowing your truck is in top condition instills confidence in your operations.

5. **Compliance with Regulations:**

   - Adhering to a Maintenance Schedule ensures that your food truck complies with safety and health regulations, preventing potential legal issues.

Maintenance Schedule is your proactive ally, ensuring your food truck not only runs smoothly but also delivers excellence at every stop. It's not just about keeping your truck in top shape; it's also a handy reference for the companies you rely on to maintain your equipment. This can be valuable information in case you ever need it.

CHAPTER 4
Event Calendar

Stay ahead of your schedule with a comprehensive event calendar. Note down festivals, gatherings, and potential hotspots where your food truck can make a mark. Planning ahead is the key to maximizing your presence.

Crafting Success: The Role of an Event Calendar in Your Food Truck Journey

Having a well-organized Event Calendar is like having a secret recipe for success. Let's explore what an Event Calendar is and uncover how it can elevate your food truck venture to new heights.

Unveiling the Event Calendar: An Event Calendar for your food truck is a strategic tool that outlines your upcoming appearances, festivals, markets, and other events where you plan to roll out your culinary delights. More than just dates and locations, it's your roadmap for navigating the diverse landscape of potential customers and ensuring that your presence is felt wherever hungry patrons gather.

Key Components of an Event Calendar:

1. **Date and Time:**
   - Clearly stating the date and time of each event ensures that you and your team are well-prepared to meet the demands of each unique occasion.

2. **Location and Address:**

   - Precise details about the event's location, including the address and any specific guidelines, help you navigate with ease and set up your food truck efficiently.

3. **Event Type:**

   - Categorizing events, whether they are festivals, farmers' markets, corporate gatherings, or private parties, allows you to tailor your menu and approach to suit the occasion.

4. **Permit and Licensing Information:**

   - Including permit details and any required licenses for each event ensures that you remain compliant with local regulations, avoiding legal hiccups.

5. **Expected Foot Traffic:**

   - Anticipating the number of attendees helps you gauge the volume of food preparation and staff required, optimizing your resources for each event.

One of the joys of the food truck community is the camaraderie when multiple trucks gather at one location. However, when considering event invitations, it's crucial to inquire about the number of participating food trucks and vendors. It's not just about quantity but also the variety of offerings. Understanding the competition is key. If an event expects 200 attendees with 16 food vendors, and six of them are offering similar products to yours, it might not be the best use of your time. This insight helps you make informed decisions and avoid poorly planned events that might not be worth your while.

How an Event Calendar Can Help:

1. **Efficient Planning:**

   - With a well-structured Event Calendar, you can plan your operations, staffing, and inventory effectively, avoiding last-minute

scrambles and ensuring a seamless experience for both you and your customers.

2. **Strategic Menu Tailoring:**

   - Knowing the nature of each event allows you to customize your menu, offering dishes that resonate with the specific audience, enhancing your chances of success.

3. **Building Anticipation:**

   - Sharing your Event Calendar with your followers builds anticipation and helps create a loyal customer base. Patrons can plan to visit your truck at their favorite events, fostering a sense of community around your brand.

4. **Optimizing Marketing Efforts:**

   - Armed with your Event Calendar, you can strategically market your participation in upcoming events, leveraging social media, local publications, and other channels to maximize visibility.

5. **Flexibility and Adaptability:**

   - An Event Calendar isn't set in stone. It allows you to adapt to changing circumstances, explore new opportunities, and adjust your schedule to align with emerging trends or unforeseen challenges.

In the dynamic realm of food truck entrepreneurship, an Event Calendar isn't just a logistical tool; it's your compass, guiding you through a flavorful journey of opportunities. Embrace it, nurture it, and let it lead you to a feast of success at every event on your horizon.

Understanding the event's theme allows you to customize your menu for a better fit. For instance, if you specialize in pasta and are invited to an Elementary School Trunk or Treat, consider offering more portable items like macaroni and cheese bites.

If adapting your menu isn't feasible, it might indicate that this event isn't the right fit for your offerings. Politely decline and suggest considering you for a more suitable occasion, such as the PTA luncheon. It's essential to maintain the integrity of your regular menu rather than hastily switching to hot dogs and pizza for the sake of a particular event— it's neither cost-effective nor a wise long-term strategy.

CHAPTER 5
Licensing and Permits Checklist

Don't let paperwork be the bane of your existence. Maintain a checklist for all necessary licenses and permits, ensuring you're always compliant with local regulations. Most of these will come around annually.

Navigating the Regulatory Landscape: The Power of a Licensing and Permits Checklist

Embarking on your food truck journey involves more than just crafting delectable dishes; it requires mastering the intricate dance of regulations and permits. A Licensing and Permits Checklist emerges as your guiding partner, ensuring you hit all the right notes in compliance. Let's delve into what this checklist entails and how it can be your compass in the regulatory labyrinth.

Decoding the Licensing and Permits Checklist: Imagine it as your comprehensive roadmap, detailing every permit, license, and inspection required to operate your food truck legally. From health permits to fire safety certifications, it encompasses the entire spectrum of regulatory requirements that vary across jurisdictions.

Key Components of a Licensing and Permits Checklist:

1. **Health Department Permits:**
   - Ensuring your food truck meets health and sanitation standards is paramount. This includes permits related to food handling, storage, and overall hygiene.

2. **Fire Safety Inspections:**

   - Fire safety is a critical aspect. Your checklist should include items such as fire extinguisher inspections and compliance with fire marshal regulations.

3. **City-Specific Licenses:**

   - Different cities may have specific licensing requirements for mobile food vendors. Your checklist should account for obtaining and renewing these licenses.

4. **State Tax License:**

   - Securing a state tax license is often a prerequisite. Your checklist should guide you through the application process, submission of necessary documents, and compliance with state tax regulations.

5. **City Tax License:**

   - Beyond state-level taxes, many cities require their own tax licenses. Your checklist should outline the steps to obtain and maintain this city-specific license.

6. **Insurance Coverage:**

   - Insurance is a safety net for unforeseen challenges. Your checklist should cover obtaining comprehensive coverage for both your food truck and the vehicle hauling it.

7. **Compliance with Zoning Laws:**

   - Zoning regulations can impact where you operate. Your checklist should include ensuring compliance with local zoning laws to avoid legal complications.

8. **Environmental Health Permits:**

   - Depending on your location, environmental health permits may be necessary. Your checklist should guide you through the process of obtaining and adhering to these permits.

How a Licensing and Permits Checklist Can Help:

1. **Preventing Legal Hassles:**

    - By systematically addressing each permit and license, you reduce the risk of legal issues that could disrupt your operations and impact your reputation.

2. **Operational Continuity:**

    - A well-maintained checklist ensures that you stay on top of renewals and expirations, preventing interruptions in your business due to expired permits.

3. **Financial Planning:**

    - Knowing the costs associated with each permit allows you to budget effectively and avoid unexpected financial burdens.

4. **Building Credibility:**

    - Displaying a commitment to compliance enhances your credibility with customers, event organizers, and local authorities, fostering positive relationships.

5. **Navigating Expansion:**

    - If you plan to operate in multiple cities or states, the checklist provides a scalable guide for navigating diverse regulatory landscapes.

In the intricate tapestry of food truck entrepreneurship, a Licensing and Permits Checklist is your secret weapon, ensuring that you not only survive but thrive within the regulatory framework. Embrace it as a fundamental tool on your path to culinary success.

CHAPTER 6
Financial Tracker

Keep tabs on your expenses, earnings, and profits. A detailed financial tracker lets you make informed decisions, steering your business toward financial success.

Mastering Finances: The Crucial Role of a Financial Tracker in Your Food Truck Venture

In the dynamic world of food truck entrepreneurship, where flavor meets finance, having a robust financial tracker is akin to wielding a precision tool for success. Let's explore the significance of a financial tracker and how it can be your ally in navigating the monetary intricacies of your culinary enterprise.

Unveiling the Financial Tracker: A financial tracker is more than just columns of numbers; it's a strategic compass that guides you through the fiscal landscape of your food truck business. At its core, it's a tool designed to record, monitor, and analyze your financial transactions, offering insights that empower informed decision-making.

Key Components of a Financial Tracker:

1. **Income and Expenses:**
   - Track every dollar flowing in and out of your business. Categorize income sources and allocate expenses meticulously to gain a clear understanding of your cash flow.

2. **Cost of Goods Sold (COGS):**

  ▪ Understand the direct costs associated with producing your culinary delights. Tracking COGS helps optimize pricing and maintain healthy profit margins.

This part is super important, and you need to get it down pat. You have to start seeing prices in a new way, especially for each thing you're planning to sell. If you don't, you're setting yourself up for failure. Mastering this skill helps you price your items just right while staying competitive. It's the key to making your food truck a hit and staying in business.

<u>*BREAKDOWN YOUR MENU ITEMS.*</u>

For example, let's say you are making a cheeseburger. And you want to charge $4.00 for that cheeseburger. Can you afford to charge $4.00?

Bun:

  • *Cost per pack: $2.94*

  • *Number of buns per pack: 8*

  • *Cost per bun: $2.94 / 8 = **$0.37***

Cheese:

  • *Cost per pack: $17.29*

  • *Number of cheese slices per pack: 120*

- *Cost per cheese slice: $17.29 / 120 = **$0.14***

Meat Patty:

- *Cost per pack: $80.95*

- *Number of meat patties per pack: 60*

- *Cost per meat patty: $80.95 / 60 = **$1.35***

Lettuce:

- *Cost per pack: $32.95*

- *Amount of lettuce per pack: 5 lbs. or 80 oz. (divide using the unit of measurement in your recipe. So, since this is lettuce your recipe probably has you using "so many" ounces, not pounds. So, we converted the pounds to ounces.*

- *Cost per serving: $32.95 / 80 = **$0.41***

Tomato:

- *Cost per item: $1.98*

- *Number of tomatoes per pack: one could yield 10 slices*

- *Cost per tomato: $1.98 / 10 = **$0.20***

Mayonnaise:

- *Cost per jar: $4.64*

- *Amount of mayonnaise used per burger: 60 TBSPS in this jar. Our recipe asks for 1 TBSP*

- *Cost per serving: $4.64 / 60 = **$0.08***

Now, let's sum it up. The total cost to make this cheeseburger is $2.55. So, you could indeed sell yours for $4.00. You have the flexibility to set your selling price strategically.

If competitors are selling similar items for $5.30, you might consider pricing yours at $5.00. However, be mindful of the local market. If competitors are selling at $3.00, it's worth reassessing your menu or exploring different suppliers. Selling it at $3.00 might not be in your best interest. Remember, pricing is a dynamic decision influenced by both cost considerations and the competitive landscape.

Here's a point worth mentioning about pricing. Some food truck owners opt to increase their prices for special events. For instance, the cheeseburger that's regularly $5.00 on a Wednesday might jump to $20 at a state fair. Personally, I find this approach questionable. It can come across as shady to loyal customers who are accustomed to your regular prices. While it's true that events may come with additional costs, like vendor fees ranging from $25 to $2000, there are more strategic ways to handle it. Consider a modest price increase, say a dollar or two, and ensure your truck is efficiently packed to handle higher volumes. This way, you recover your costs and more, all while maintaining the loyalty of all your customers.

3. **Operating Costs:**

   - Beyond ingredients, factor in all operational expenses, from fuel and maintenance to licensing fees and insurance. A comprehensive overview ensures no cost is overlooked.

4. **Tax Obligations:**

   - Keep a vigilant eye on your tax liabilities. A financial tracker aids in setting aside funds for taxes, preventing unpleasant surprises during tax season.

5. **Profit and Loss Statements:**

   ▪ Generate regular profit and loss statements to evaluate the overall financial health of your venture. Identify trends and areas for improvement to enhance profitability.

6. **Budget Planning:**

   ▪ Develop and adhere to a budget. A financial tracker facilitates proactive budget planning, allowing you to allocate resources efficiently and avoid unnecessary expenditures.

How a Financial Tracker Can Help:

1. **Informed Decision-Making:**

   ▪ Access to real-time financial data empowers you to make informed decisions promptly, steering your business toward sustainable growth.

2. **Expense Control:**

   ▪ Identify areas of excessive spending or operational inefficiencies. A financial tracker acts as a diagnostic tool, enabling you to optimize costs without compromising quality.

3. **Tax Compliance:**

   ▪ Stay on top of tax obligations with organized financial records. A financial tracker simplifies the process of filing taxes and ensures compliance with regulatory requirements.

4. **Business Viability Assessment:**

   ▪ Regularly assess the viability of your food truck venture. Analyze profit margins, assess the impact of pricing changes, and pivot your strategy based on financial insights.

5. **Investor Relations:**

   - If seeking investors or loans, a well-maintained financial tracker enhances your credibility. It demonstrates diligence in financial management and instills confidence in potential partners.

6. **Long-Term Planning:**

   - Plan for the future with confidence. A financial tracker aids in forecasting and long-term financial planning, helping you set realistic goals and milestones for your business.

In the realm of food truck entrepreneurship, where precision and flavor intertwine, a financial tracker is your compass, guiding you toward fiscal success. Embrace it as an indispensable companion on your journey to culinary triumph.

CHAPTER 7
Supplier Contacts

Your suppliers are your lifeline. Create a comprehensive contact list with details of your suppliers for ingredients, packaging, and other essentials. A quick reference when you need to restock in a hurry.

Navigating the Culinary Ecosystem: The Significance of Supplier Contacts in Your Food Truck Odyssey

The relationships you forge with suppliers can be the secret sauce to your success. Let's delve into the importance of maintaining robust supplier contacts and how they can elevate your food truck venture to new heights.

The Essence of Supplier Contacts: Supplier contacts go beyond mere transactions; they are the lifeline of your culinary enterprise. These relationships extend to those providing you with fresh produce, quality meats, essential kitchen supplies, and everything in between. Here's why nurturing these connections is pivotal:

1. **Reliability and Consistency:**
   - Establishing solid relationships with suppliers ensures a steady and consistent flow of high-quality ingredients. Reliability is key in meeting customer expectations and maintaining the integrity of your menu.

2. **Negotiating Power:**

   - A network of trusted supplier contacts gives you negotiating power. Whether it's negotiating prices, bulk discounts, or favorable credit terms, strong relationships empower you to secure the best deals for your business.

3. **Adaptability to Seasonal Changes:**

   - Culinary trends and ingredient availability can vary with seasons. Maintaining open communication with suppliers enables you to adapt your menu to seasonal changes, keeping your offerings fresh and in demand.

4. **Timely Updates on Market Trends:**

   - Suppliers are plugged into market trends. Regular communication with them provides valuable insights into emerging culinary trends, allowing you to stay ahead of the curve and captivate your customers with innovative offerings.

5. **Emergency Preparedness:**

   - Unforeseen circumstances, such as supply chain disruptions, can impact your business. Strong relationships with suppliers facilitate effective communication during emergencies, helping you navigate challenges seamlessly.

How Supplier Contacts Can Help:

1. **Quality Assurance:**

   - Direct communication with suppliers ensures that you receive top-notch ingredients. This quality assurance translates into the exceptional taste and consistency that keep customers coming back for more.

2. **Cost-Efficiency:**

   - Negotiate better prices and terms by cultivating strong supplier contacts. Cost-efficiency is crucial in maximizing profits, and collaborative relationships with suppliers contribute to achieving this goal.

3. **Menu Innovation:**

    ▪ Stay abreast of culinary trends and innovations by tapping into your supplier network. Access to new and exciting ingredients allows you to continuously evolve your menu, captivating customers with fresh and enticing offerings.

4. **Mitigating Risks:**

    ▪ A diversified network of suppliers reduces the risk of disruptions. If one supplier faces challenges, you can seamlessly source ingredients from alternative contacts, ensuring uninterrupted operations.

5. **Building Trust and Loyalty:**

    ▪ Trust is the cornerstone of lasting partnerships. By maintaining transparent and mutually beneficial relationships with suppliers, you build trust and loyalty that can lead to long-term collaborations and preferential treatment.

In the intricate dance of flavors and logistics, supplier contacts are your trusted dance partners. Nurturing these relationships enhances the resilience, innovation, and profitability of your food truck venture, making them an indispensable asset on your culinary journey.

CHAPTER 8
Menu Performance Tracker

Analyze the performance of your menu items. Identify best-sellers and underperformers, allowing you to fine-tune your offerings based on customer preferences.

Menu Symphony: The Impact of a Menu Performance Tracker in Orchestrating Culinary Success

In the gastronomic ballet of a food truck, the menu isn't just a list of dishes; it's a dynamic composition that can either steal the spotlight or fade into the background. Enter the Menu Performance Tracker – a virtuoso tool that fine-tunes your menu, ensuring each dish resonates with your audience and contributes to the crescendo of your culinary success.

Decoding the Essence of Menu Performance Tracking: A Menu Performance Tracker is your backstage pass to the intricacies of your food truck's culinary performance. It's more than numbers; it's a strategic lens through which you can optimize your menu for maximum impact. Here's why this tracker is a maestro in the symphony of your culinary offerings:

1. **Identifying All-Stars and Underdogs:**
   - Not all dishes are created equal. A Menu Performance Tracker dissects the popularity of each item on your menu. Identify the shining stars that have customers coming back for more and pinpoint the underperformers that might need a revamp or strategic promotion.

2. **Seasonal Sensibility:**

   - Culinary trends and preferences change with the seasons. The tracker helps you discern seasonal fluctuations in the popularity of dishes. Leverage this information to introduce seasonal specials or make adjustments to your menu that align with customer cravings throughout the year.

3. **Pricing Precision:**

   - The tracker provides insights into the correlation between pricing and customer choices. Optimize your pricing strategy by understanding which price points resonate with your audience, ensuring your menu is not just delectable but also economically enticing.

4. **Strategic Innovation:**

   - Innovate with purpose. The tracker allows you to experiment with new dishes or variations, guided by real-time data on customer responses. This strategic innovation keeps your menu dynamic, offering fresh experiences that captivate your audience.

5. **Combo Coordination:**

   - Uncover the magic of pairings. A Menu Performance Tracker helps you identify successful dish combinations, allowing you to create enticing combos that maximize sales and customer satisfaction. Whether it's a perfect duo of flavors or a well-balanced meal deal, the tracker guides your combo creations.

How a Menu Performance Tracker Can Help:

1. **Optimizing Menu Composition:**

   - Fine-tune your menu based on performance data. Highlight and promote customer favorites, consider revamping or repositioning underperforming dishes, and ensure a well-balanced and attractive menu composition.

2. **Data-Driven Decision Making:**

   - Make informed decisions backed by real-time data. The tracker empowers you to pivot your menu strategy with confidence, aligning your offerings with customer preferences and market trends.

3. **Maximizing Revenue Streams:**

   - Identify high-margin dishes and strategic pricing points to maximize revenue. The tracker helps you uncover opportunities to enhance profitability without compromising on customer satisfaction.

4. **Adapting to Trends:**

   - Stay ahead of culinary trends by adapting your menu in response to changing customer preferences. The tracker acts as your compass, guiding you through the ever-evolving landscape of gastronomic desires.

5. **Enhancing Customer Satisfaction:**

   - A well-curated menu, shaped by insights from the tracker, translates to heightened customer satisfaction. Satisfied customers are not just patrons; they become brand ambassadors, contributing to the long-term success of your food truck.

In the symphony of flavors, the Menu Performance Tracker is the conductor, orchestrating a harmonious blend of customer delight and culinary brilliance. Utilize this tool to compose a menu that resonates with your audience, ensuring that every bite is a note in the grand melody of your food truck's success.

Remember, these files and trackers aren't just paperwork; they are the pillars supporting your food truck venture. Stay organized, stay ahead!

CHAPTER 9
Event Details and Management

Mastering the Rhythm of Success: The Art of Event Application and Details Management

In the culinary symphony of your food truck business, each event is a unique movement, and orchestrating them seamlessly requires a well-tuned system for handling event applications. This involves not only securing the necessary paperwork, such as the Certificate of Liability Insurance (COI) but also delving into the specifics of each event. Let's unravel the intricacies of this process:

1. **Event Invitation Intelligence:**

   - When the invitation to an event comes knocking, it's not just about saying yes; it's about understanding the entire composition of the event. Develop a comprehensive system to gather crucial details from event organizers, including the date, time, expected crowd size, and the number of fellow vendors in attendance.

2. **Strategic Product Planning:**

   - Armed with event details, you gain insight into the scale and nature of the gathering. This is invaluable for strategic product planning. Knowing the expected crowd helps you estimate the quantity of food and supplies to prepare, ensuring you're well-equipped to meet demand without overstocking.

3. Historical Insight for Future Success:

- Keeping meticulous records of past events is akin to having a musical score for each performance. If you've participated in the same event before, historical data becomes your guide. Track what worked well in terms of sales, popular menu items, and logistical considerations. This historical insight allows you to make informed adjustments for a more harmonious and successful encore.

4. Adaptability in Action:

- Events vary in size, theme, and audience, and your adaptability is key to delivering a pitch-perfect performance every time. With a system in place for handling event details, you can tailor your offerings to align with the unique characteristics of each event, ensuring a customized and memorable experience for attendees.

5. Building Lasting Impressions:

- Beyond the culinary delights, the success of your food truck at an event hinges on the overall experience you provide. Managing event details allows you to anticipate logistical challenges, coordinate effectively with event organizers, and create a seamless and enjoyable experience for both your team and customers.

How Event Application Management Enhances Your Symphony:

1. Efficiency in Planning:

- Streamline your preparation process by having all event details at your fingertips. This efficiency translates to smoother logistics, reduced stress, and an overall well-orchestrated participation in events.

2. Strategic Decision-Making:

- Armed with historical data and current event details, you can make strategic decisions on menu offerings, pricing, and staffing. This proactive approach positions your food truck for success in diverse event scenarios.

3. **Customer-Centric Approach:**

- Understanding the unique aspects of each event allows you to tailor your menu and service to the preferences of the audience. This customer-centric approach fosters positive interactions and encourages repeat business.

4. **Data-Driven Growth:**

- Over time, the data collected from various events becomes a treasure trove for growth. Analyze patterns, identify trends, and use this data to refine your strategies, expanding your reach and impact in the ever-evolving landscape of culinary events.

In the grand composition of your food truck's success, mastering the art of event application and details management is like conducting a symphony with precision and flair. Be the maestro of your culinary destiny, orchestrating each event with finesse and creating a harmonious experience that resonates with both your team and the delighted audience.

CHAPTER 10
Tax Wisdom

Smart Tax Choreography: Embracing Daily or Weekly Payments

In the intricate dance of financial management for your food truck venture, the spotlight now turns to the rhythm of tax payments. Let's explore the benefits and practicality of making your tax payments online on a daily or weekly basis—a strategic move that can turn a potentially overwhelming task into a manageable routine.

1. Daily or Weekly: The Psychological Advantage:

- Imagine a daily tax payment as a series of light, manageable steps, contrasting with the weight of a lump sum at month-end. The psychological advantage is clear: parting with smaller amounts regularly is easier on the entrepreneur's mindset and financial flow.

2. Taming the Financial Rollercoaster:

- By opting for daily or weekly payments, you transform the unpredictable financial rollercoaster into a controlled ride. This approach ensures that your business stays on top of its tax obligations without the stress of accumulating a significant amount by month-end.

3. Seamless Integration with Operations:

- Incorporating online tax payments into your daily or weekly routine seamlessly integrates this financial chore with your operational processes. Utilize modern Point-of-Sale (POS) systems or online platforms to streamline the payment process, making it a natural part of your business workflow.

4. Disciplined Financial Management:

- Making frequent tax payments online reflects a commitment to disciplined financial management. It eliminates the risk of forgetting or procrastinating until the last moment. This proactive approach aligns with the rhythm of your business, promoting a sense of control over your financial responsibilities.

5. The Technical How-To:

- Online tax payments are often facilitated through the tax authority's official website. Identify the option for making payments and explore whether daily or weekly schedules are supported. With a few clicks, you can contribute smaller amounts consistently, keeping your tax obligations in check.

6. Leverage Technology for Convenience:

- Embrace the convenience of technology. If your business relies on a POS system, leverage its capabilities to calculate daily tax amounts. For businesses without a POS, manual calculations can be performed, ensuring accuracy before making online payments.

7. The Long-Term Benefits:

- Consistency in daily or weekly tax payments not only eases the immediate financial burden but also sets the stage for long-term stability. It fosters a proactive mindset, aligning your business with financial responsibility and ensuring a smooth, sustainable tax management process.

In the symphony of financial mastery for your food truck venture, the choice to pay taxes daily or weekly emerges as a harmonious note. By embracing this strategic approach, you not only alleviate the stress associated with lump-sum payments but also establish a disciplined rhythm that resonates with the heartbeat of your business. Welcome to the cadence of financial finesse—a key element in your journey to food truck prosperity.

You'll find more practical tax tips in *CHAPTER 13: BANK ACCOUNTS AND FINANCIAL WISDOM.*

CHAPTER 11
Receipts And More

Receipts, Vendors, and More: The Bedrock of Financial Accountability

In the intricate dance of food truck entrepreneurship, maintaining meticulous records is not just a bureaucratic chore; it's the bedrock of financial accountability. The synergy of receipts, vendors, repairs, contracts, and insurance documents forms a tapestry of information that, when woven together seamlessly, becomes a powerful tool for steering your business toward success. Let's explore why keeping track of these elements is indispensable and how technology can be a game-changer in preserving those small but crucial receipts.

1. Expense Tracking and Financial Clarity:

- *Receipts:* Every crumpled receipt is a piece of the financial puzzle. Keeping track of all your receipts, whether for ingredients, fuel, or equipment, provides a comprehensive view of your expenses. This meticulous record-keeping is not just about compliance; it's about gaining clarity on where your money is going and making informed decisions to optimize spending.

2. Vendor Relationships and Quality Control:

- *Vendors:* Your choice of vendors can significantly impact the quality and cost of your supplies. Maintaining a record of vendor interactions, agreements, and invoices ensures transparency and accountability. It also aids in evaluating vendor performance and allows you to make informed decisions about the suppliers you want to continue working with.

3. Operational Integrity and Repairs:

- *Repairs:* Food truck operations can encounter wear and tear. Keeping a detailed record of repairs is crucial for operational integrity. It helps in identifying patterns, planning for preventive maintenance, and budgeting for unforeseen repairs. Additionally, having a repair history is valuable when assessing the overall health of your food truck.

4. Legal Safeguard and Contracts:

- *Contracts:* Contracts are the backbone of business agreements. Whether it's agreements with event organizers, collaborations, or partnerships, having a documented record of contracts is essential for legal safeguarding. It clarifies expectations, protects your interests, and provides a reference point in case of disputes.

5. Compliance and Insurance Documentation:

- *Insurance Documents:* In the unpredictable world of food truck operations, insurance is your safety net. Accidents, damages, or unforeseen events can disrupt business. Keeping insurance documents in order ensures that you are compliant with legal requirements and provides a quick reference in case of emergencies.

The Tech Advantage: Taming the Paper Trail:

- In the digital era, technology emerges as a powerful ally in managing the intricacies of record-keeping, especially when dealing with countless small receipts. Consider these tech-savvy approaches:
  - *Expense Tracking Apps:* Utilize mobile apps designed for expense tracking. Snap photos of your receipts, categorize them and store them digitally. This not only reduces paper clutter but also streamlines the process of accessing and organizing your expenses.

o   *Cloud Storage:* Embrace cloud storage solutions to safeguard important documents. Cloud platforms provide secure and accessible storage, ensuring that your records are not vulnerable to physical damage or loss.

o   *Digital Contracts:* Opt for digital contract management tools. These platforms allow you to create, store, and manage contracts digitally, facilitating easy retrieval and reducing the risk of misplaced or damaged paperwork.

The Tapestry of Success:

- In the grand tapestry of food truck entrepreneurship, the threads of receipts, vendors, repairs, contracts, and insurance documents are woven with precision. This tapestry not only serves as a historical record but also as a compass for navigating the financial landscape of your business. Embrace the art of record-keeping, for within its details lies the roadmap to informed decisions, financial stability, and the enduring success of your food truck venture.

In a nutshell, make sure to keep both hard copy files and digital records for all ten areas we've covered. This meticulous approach to documenting your business will not only serve you well in the present but can also become a valuable asset if you ever decide to sell your brand in the future. It's a key element in maintaining and ensuring your success.

Food Truck Start Guide Checklist.docx

CHAPTER 12
Customer Feedback Log

Feedback is gold. Keep a log of customer comments, suggestions, and reviews. It's not just about improvement; it's about building a community around your culinary creations.

Harvesting Success: The Role of Customer Feedback Logs in Cultivating a Thriving Food Truck Business

In the dynamic world of food truck entrepreneurship, customer feedback isn't just a review; it's a strategic tool that can shape the trajectory of your success. Let's explore the significance of maintaining comprehensive Customer Feedback Logs and how they can be the compass guiding your culinary venture toward excellence.

Unlocking the Essence of Customer Feedback Logs: Customer Feedback Logs are more than a collection of comments; they are a treasure trove of insights into your customers' preferences, expectations, and overall satisfaction. Here's why these logs are indispensable to your food truck odyssey:

1. **Insight into Preferences:**
   - Customer feedback unveils the preferences and tastes that resonate with your audience. Understanding what dishes or flavors receive positive responses empowers you to tailor your menu to align with customer expectations.

2. **Identifying Improvement Areas:**

   - Honest feedback provides a roadmap for improvement. By acknowledging areas that may need enhancement, you can refine your culinary offerings, service, or overall experience, ensuring a continuous evolution toward excellence.

3. **Enhancing Customer Experience:**

   - Positive feedback highlights aspects of your business that customers appreciate. Leveraging this information allows you to amplify those elements, creating a consistently delightful experience that fosters customer loyalty.

4. **Nurturing Customer Relationships:**

   - Responding to feedback, whether positive or constructive, showcases your commitment to customer satisfaction. This engagement builds a connection with your audience, fostering loyalty and turning one-time customers into repeat patrons.

5. **Adapting to Trends:**

   - Customer preferences evolve, and your food truck must evolve with them. Feedback logs act as a barometer for emerging trends, enabling you to adapt your menu or services to stay current and enticing to your target audience.

How Customer Feedback Logs Can Help:

1. **Continuous Improvement:**

   - Regularly reviewing feedback logs allows you to identify patterns and trends. This insight enables continuous improvement, ensuring that your food truck remains a dynamic and evolving culinary destination.

2. **Tailoring Offerings:**

   - Customize your menu based on feedback to meet the evolving tastes of your customers. By offering dishes that resonate with them, you create a personalized and memorable experience, setting your food truck apart.

3. **Building Reputation:**

   - Positive feedback contributes to building a stellar reputation. Customer testimonials, shared on social media or your website, become powerful marketing tools that attract new customers and reinforce your brand's credibility.

4. **Swift Issue Resolution:**

   - Promptly addressing concerns raised in feedback logs demonstrates your commitment to customer satisfaction. Swift issue resolution turns potential negative experiences into positive ones, salvaging customer relationships and loyalty.

5. **Innovating with Confidence:**

   - Armed with insights from feedback logs, you can innovate with confidence. Introduce new dishes, services, or experiences backed by a deep understanding of what your customers desire, positioning your food truck as a trendsetter.

In the symphony of flavors and customer interactions, Customer Feedback Logs are the sheet music guiding your performance. Harnessing the power of these logs elevates your food truck venture, transforming it into a harmonious blend of customer satisfaction and culinary excellence.

CHAPTER 13
Bank Accounts and Financial Wisdom

Navigating the Fiscal Landscape: Bank Accounts, Taxes, and Financial Wisdom

Embarking on the entrepreneurial journey of owning a food truck involves not just savoring the flavors but also mastering the intricate dance of finances. Let's dive into the labyrinth of bank accounts and taxes, demystifying the often overlooked yet critical realm of financial management.

1. The Tax Wake-Up Call:

- Taxes, the formidable force that catches many entrepreneurs off guard. In the world of food trucks, it's not a once-a-year affair; it's a monthly or quarterly tango. The realization dawned on us when an email was received, signaling overdue taxes. The lesson? Monthly or quarterly tax obligations are the norm; ensure you know your category.

2. Daily Tax Choreography:

- To tame the tax beast, incorporate a daily routine. Whether through a Point-of-Sale (POS) system or manual calculations, segregate the daily tax collection. It's a psychological game: parting with $40 daily is easier than facing a hefty $1400 bill later. If you don't have a POS, manually calculate, and deposit the tax into a designated account named—aptly—'taxes.'

3. Disciplined Deposits:

- Create a separate checking account for taxes, fostering discipline and clarity. Modern banking allows easy setup through online platforms. As funds accumulate, the account becomes a reservoir for squaring up with the government. The key is disciplined separation, ensuring tax money is not mingled with operational funds. Remember, this isn't your money; it's the tax the customer already paid, and your role is to safeguard it until it's time to hand it over to the government. Make sure not to mix this up!

- Now, if you've chosen not to include tax in your item prices and intend to calculate it later, that's okay. However, it's crucial to consistently calculate and set aside the required tax amount either daily or, at the very least, weekly. Don't wait until the end of the month to discover a surprising tax bill. Be proactive and ensure you're regularly putting aside the necessary funds into your tax account. It will hurt your feelings far less this way!

4. Balancing Act:

- Two approaches govern the tax balancing act. Either wait till month-end or quarter-end for a consolidated payment, breaking down city and state taxes. Alternatively, if discipline is your forte, make daily or weekly payments to prevent a financial jolt. The objective is a seamless reconciliation at filing time, avoiding a stressful financial rollercoaster.

5. Additional Financial Arsenal:

- Beyond the tax saga, consider setting up two additional accounts: profit and growth. The profit account serves as the reservoir for your hard-earned gains, while the growth account fuels your business's expansion. A suggested formula is allocating 50% of profits to the growth account, fostering a balance between reward and reinvestment.

6. Filing Rituals:

- Regularly file your taxes within the designated period, updating gross amounts, tax collections, and other required information. Print and diligently store forms and payment history in your financial archives, building a comprehensive record for future reference.

7. Profit and Growth Alchemy:

- Unveiling the secret sauce of financial success lies in discerning your profit. A later discussion will unravel the method. The growth account, on the other hand, becomes a reservoir for reinvestment, enabling your food truck to thrive and evolve.

As you navigate the financial waters of your food truck venture, consider this your compass. The intricate steps of managing bank accounts, taxes, and financial growth may seem daunting, but with disciplined choreography, you'll find a rhythm that propels your business toward sustained success.

CHAPTER 14
Growth Account

The Growth Account: Nurturing Prosperity for Your Food Truck Venture

In the orchestration of financial strategies for your food truck business, the concept of a Growth Account emerges as a key instrument. This specialized account serves as a sanctuary for cultivating the seeds of future success, offering a structured approach to managing your finances and fostering sustainable growth. Let's delve into what a Growth Account entails and how it becomes a powerful ally in steering your business toward prosperity.

Defining the Growth Account:

- A Growth Account is a designated financial reservoir within your business framework. Its purpose is twofold: to safeguard profits and to allocate a portion for strategic reinvestment into the business. Think of it as a nurturing garden where financial seeds are planted, cultivated, and eventually harvested for sustained growth.

How It Works:

- The Growth Account operates on a simple principle: allocate a predetermined percentage of your profits to this account. For instance, earmarking 50% of your profits for growth is a common practice. This disciplined approach ensures that a substantial portion of your earnings is preserved for future initiatives, shielding it from daily operational expenses.

Managing Finances Effectively:

- By segregating a portion of profits into the Growth Account, you create a financial boundary between operational funds and growth capital. This segregation is crucial for effective financial management. It prevents the temptation to dip into funds earmarked for growth, promoting a disciplined approach to expenditure.

Benefits of a Growth Account:

- *Financial Discipline:* The Growth Account instills financial discipline by ring-fencing a portion of profits. This separation helps maintain clarity on available resources for daily operations versus those earmarked for expansion.

- *Strategic Reinvestment:* The accumulated funds in the Growth Account serve as strategic capital for reinvestment. Whether it's upgrading equipment, expanding your menu, or exploring new locations, these funds provide the financial foundation for calculated growth.

- *Emergency Cushion:* Beyond growth initiatives, the Growth Account acts as an emergency cushion. Unforeseen expenses or opportunities can be addressed without jeopardizing the core operational budget.

- *Long-Term Sustainability:* A Growth Account fosters long-term sustainability. It ensures that your business is not just thriving in the present but is strategically positioning itself for sustained success and relevance in the future.

Saving for Growth, One Transaction at a Time:

- Imagine every profitable transaction contributing to the growth of your business. By consistently channeling a portion of earnings into the Growth Account, you create a reservoir that holds the potential for transformative expansions, innovative ventures, and enduring success.

The Financial Sanctuary for Tomorrow's Triumphs:

- In the dynamic world of food truck entrepreneurship, the Growth Account stands as a sanctuary for tomorrow's triumphs. It's not just about saving money;

it's about cultivating a mindset of sustainable growth. By embracing the Growth Account, you lay the groundwork for a prosperous future, ensuring that your food truck venture not only survives but thrives in the ever-evolving landscape of culinary entrepreneurship.

CHAPTER 15
Locations for Setup

Locations: A Strategic Guide to Parking Your Success

In the dynamic world of food truck entrepreneurship, the right location can be the secret ingredient that transforms your venture from good to gourmet. Whether you're seeking daily work spots or eye-catching event locations, mastering the art of securing prime real estate for your food truck is a skill worth honing. Let's delve into the strategies for finding the perfect locations to park your mobile culinary haven.

1. Street Traffic Visibility: Be Seen, Be Safe:

- *Strategic Visibility:* Position yourself where street traffic is bustling, ensuring that your food truck becomes a beacon of temptation for passersby. However, always prioritize safety for both you and your customers. Seek locations with high foot traffic and visibility to maximize your reach.

- *Certificate of Liability Insurance (COI):* Some locations may require proof of insurance in the form of a Certificate of Liability Insurance (COI). Check local regulations and be prepared to provide this document to secure sought-after spots.

2. Daily Work Locations: Diversify Your Presence:

- *Strategic Variety:* To keep your food truck operational on a daily basis, consider a diverse array of locations. Explore options such as service stations, auto part stores, grocery stores, beauty supply stores, pawn shops, RV parks, and locally-owned businesses. This variety not only expands your reach but also introduces your culinary delights to different demographics.

- *City Hall Permissions:* Before setting up shop in these locations, check with City Hall to determine if any permissions or licenses are required. Different municipalities may have specific regulations governing mobile food vendors, and obtaining the necessary approvals ensures compliance with local laws.

3. Negotiating with Property Owners: Securing Your Space:

- *Engage with Property Owners:* In the pursuit of daily work locations, consider approaching property owners directly. Explain your business model, the benefits you bring to the community, and your commitment to cleanliness and safety. Establishing a direct relationship with property owners can lead to mutually beneficial agreements.

- *Written Permissions:* Whether you're parking on an abandoned lot or a property where the owner is not physically present, it's wise to get written permission. Even if a fee is not required, having a document that clearly states you have the owner's consent can prevent confusion or complaints from neighbors. Some cities may even require such agreements, and having them notarized adds an extra layer of credibility.

4. Compliance and Documentation: Navigating City Requirements:

- *City Requirements:* Some cities mandate that food truck operators secure written permission from property owners for their chosen locations. Check local regulations to understand specific requirements, and ensure that you comply with all necessary documentation.

- *Notarization:* In certain jurisdictions, having the written permission document notarized adds a level of formality and legality. It serves as a clear and official record of the property owner's consent, reducing potential disputes or challenges.

The Art of Location Mastery:

- As you embark on the quest for the perfect food truck locations, remember that each spot is an opportunity to showcase your culinary prowess. Be strategic, engage with property owners, navigate city requirements, and document your agreements. In the tapestry of your food truck journey, the right locations are the vibrant threads that weave a narrative of success.

Master this art and watch your food truck flourish in the diverse landscapes of daily work and special events alike.

This section primarily revolves around your day-to-day operations, those moments when you're hitting the streets to boost your brand visibility and earn some income. While certain aspects may be relevant to events, it's crucial to grasp that different gigs come with different prerequisites. For your regular work routine, ensure you've got all the permits in check, as we discussed back in Chapter 1.

Additionally, seek permission from the property owner where you plan to set up. Please, resist the urge to just park anywhere because other food trucks are doing it. Take the high road – get that permission. If they say no and point out that those other trucks aren't supposed to be there, accept it gracefully and move on. Let's keep the food truck community's reputation positive; we want people to see us as a welcome sight, not a bother.

Here are some samples. Make them your own.

[Request for Permission to Operate Food Truck on Your Property.docx](#)

[Food Truck Operation Permission Confirmation.docx](#)

Put together a packing list. You'll be tweaking and adjusting this list during the initial 30 days, depending on how frequently you hit the road. The idea is to create a baseline, but you'll likely discover a thing or two that deserves a permanent spot on your truck, or perhaps realize you've been packing a bit too much.

The goal here is to help you load your truck efficiently. Imagine being 30 miles away and realizing you forgot gloves, spoons for dipping, or those crucial to-go boxes. Here's a sample packing list – make it yours.

[Packing List.xlsx](#)

CHAPTER 16
Health and Safety Compliance

Health and Safety Compliance for Your Food Truck Business

Ensuring health and safety compliance is not just a legal requirement but a fundamental aspect of running a successful and reputable food truck business. From food handling to cleanliness standards, adhering to health department regulations is crucial for both your customers' well-being and the longevity of your venture.

1. Food Handling Guidelines:

- **Safe Food Practices:** Implement safe food handling practices to prevent contamination and ensure the safety of the food you serve. This includes proper storage, cooking temperatures, and avoiding cross-contamination.

- **Employee Training:** Train your staff on food safety protocols. This includes educating them on hygiene practices, proper handwashing techniques, and the importance of using gloves and utensils when handling food.

2. Cleanliness Standards:

- **Regular Cleaning Schedule:** Maintain a rigorous cleaning schedule for your food truck. This involves daily cleaning of cooking surfaces, utensils, and storage areas. Regular deep cleaning is also essential to prevent the buildup of grease and dirt.

- **Sanitization Practices:** Use approved sanitizers for cleaning surfaces. Regularly sanitize high-touch areas, such as door handles, payment terminals, and serving counters, to prevent the spread of germs.

3. Protocols for Compliance:

- **Health Department Requirements:** Stay informed about the specific health department requirements in your operating location. Each jurisdiction may have slightly different regulations, and compliance is essential to avoid fines or closures.

- **Regular Inspections:** Proactively schedule and participate in regular health department inspections. This not only ensures compliance but also demonstrates your commitment to maintaining high standards of cleanliness and safety.

4. Importance of Compliance:

- **Customer Trust:** Compliance with health and safety regulations builds trust with your customers. They need assurance that the food they are consuming is prepared in a safe and sanitary environment.

- **Legal Obligations:** Non-compliance can result in severe consequences, including fines, closure of the food truck, and damage to your business's reputation. Staying on top of regulations helps you avoid these pitfalls.

5. Allergen Awareness:

- **Clear Labeling:** Clearly label menu items with allergen information. This is not only a regulatory requirement but also ensures the safety of customers with food allergies.

- **Staff Training:** Train your staff to handle customer inquiries about allergens. They should be knowledgeable about the ingredients used in each dish.

6. COVID-19 Considerations:

- **Adaptation to Guidelines:** In the post-pandemic landscape, adapt your food truck operations to comply with any additional health and safety guidelines related to COVID-19. This may include measures such as contactless payment options and enhanced sanitization practices.

In summary, prioritizing health and safety compliance is an investment in the success and sustainability of your food truck business. It not only safeguards the well-being of your customers but also establishes your brand as one that takes responsibility for delivering food safely and hygienically.

CHAPTER 17
Employee Management

Employee Management for Your Food Truck Business

Managing employees in your food truck business is a critical aspect of ensuring smooth operations and delivering excellent customer service. Here's an expanded look into various aspects of employee management:

1. Hiring Processes:

- **Define Roles Clearly:** Clearly outline the roles and responsibilities for each position in your food truck, whether it's cooking, taking orders, or handling cash. This ensures that potential hires understand what is expected of them.

- **Skills Assessment:** Conduct thorough interviews and, if applicable, practical assessments to gauge the skills of potential employees. Look for individuals with relevant experience and a passion for the food industry.

2. Training:

- **Comprehensive Onboarding:** Develop a comprehensive onboarding process for new hires. This should include training on food safety, customer service, and the specific processes and equipment used in your food truck.

- **Continuous Training:** Implement ongoing training programs to keep employees updated on new menu items, safety protocols, and any changes

- in operations. Regular training enhances their skills and ensures consistency in service.

3. Scheduling:

- **Efficient Shift Planning:** Create efficient shift schedules that consider peak hours, special events, and employee availability. This ensures that you have adequate staff during busy periods.

- **Flexibility:** If possible, offer flexibility in scheduling to accommodate employees' preferences and personal commitments. A happy and well-balanced team contributes positively to the overall work environment.

4. Fostering a Positive Work Environment:

- **Team Building:** Organize team-building activities to foster camaraderie among your staff. A positive work environment contributes to better teamwork and customer service.

- **Open Communication:** Encourage open communication between you and your employees. Regularly check in with them to address concerns, gather feedback, and ensure that everyone feels heard and valued.

5. Employee Recognition:

- **Acknowledgment of Efforts:** Recognize and acknowledge the hard work and dedication of your employees. This can be done through verbal praise, employee of the month programs, or other forms of appreciation.

- **Incentives:** Consider implementing incentive programs to motivate your team. This could involve bonuses for achieving sales targets or providing exceptional customer service.

6. Adhering to Employment Laws:

- **Legal Compliance:** Ensure that your employment practices comply with local employment laws. This includes adhering to minimum wage requirements, providing breaks as mandated, and addressing any other legal obligations.

7. Cross-Training:

- **Versatility in Roles:** Cross-train your employees to handle multiple roles within the food truck. This ensures flexibility in scheduling and operations, especially during peak times or when certain team members are unavailable.

8. Conflict Resolution:

- **Establish Protocols:** Have clear protocols in place for handling conflicts or issues within the team. Address conflicts promptly and impartially to maintain a harmonious work environment.

Effective employee management contributes not only to the efficiency of your food truck but also to the overall customer experience. By investing in hiring, training, and maintaining a positive work environment, you create a team that is dedicated, skilled, and aligned with the success of your food truck business.

Strategic Growth and Engagement

CHAPTER 18
Chamber of Commerce

Harnessing Success through Local Chamber of Commerce: A Business Boost

The local Chamber of Commerce stands as a beacon for small businesses, offering a myriad of advantages that can propel your food truck venture to new heights. Joining your Chamber of Commerce is not just a formality; it's a strategic move that can open doors to opportunities, networking, and community support. Let's delve into why becoming a member of your local Chamber of Commerce is a savvy decision for the growth and prosperity of your small food truck business.

1. What is the Chamber of Commerce?

- *Community Hub:* The Chamber of Commerce is a community organization that brings together local businesses, professionals, and civic leaders. It serves as a hub for networking, collaboration, and collective efforts to enhance the economic vitality of the community.

- *Advocacy Platform:* Chambers of Commerce often play a role in advocating for the interests of businesses at local, regional, and sometimes even national levels. They voice concerns, champion initiatives, and work towards creating a conducive environment for business growth.

2. Networking Opportunities: Building Bridges, Breaking Barriers:

- *Business Connections:* Joining the Chamber of Commerce opens doors to invaluable networking opportunities. Connect with fellow business owners, professionals, and community leaders. These connections can lead to partnerships, collaborations, and shared resources that benefit your food truck business.

- *Community Engagement:* Engaging with the local business community fosters a sense of camaraderie and mutual support. Attend Chamber events, participate in forums, and showcase your food truck at local gatherings to strengthen your ties within the community.

3. Marketing and Visibility: Amplifying Your Presence:

- *Business Directory Inclusion:* Many Chambers maintain business directories that include member businesses. This inclusion enhances your food truck's visibility, making it easier for locals and potential clients to discover and engage with your services.

- *Event Sponsorship and Participation:* Chambers often organize events, festivals, and promotions. As a member, you may have opportunities to sponsor or participate in these activities, gaining exposure and reaching a broader audience.

4. Resources and Support: A Lifeline for Small Businesses:

- *Educational Programs:* Chambers frequently offer educational programs, workshops, and seminars to empower businesses with knowledge and skills. Stay informed about industry trends, best practices, and business strategies through these valuable resources.

- *Advocacy and Support:* In times of challenges or when facing regulatory issues, the Chamber of Commerce can be a powerful advocate. Leverage their support in navigating bureaucratic processes, accessing resources, and addressing concerns that impact your food truck business.

5. Community Trust and Credibility: A Seal of Approval:

- *Chamber Membership Seal:* Being a Chamber member adds a layer of credibility to your food truck business. It signifies your commitment to the local community and adherence to ethical business practices. This seal of approval can instill trust among customers and partners.

- *Community Recognition:* Chamber membership is often recognized and respected within the community. It positions your food truck as an integral part of the local business landscape, fostering positive relationships with customers and fellow entrepreneurs.

Making the Move: Joining Your Local Chamber of Commerce:

- Research your local Chamber of Commerce and explore the benefits they offer. Once you decide to join, actively participate in Chamber activities, engage with fellow members, and seize the opportunities that arise. Your food truck is not just a mobile culinary delight; it's a vital contributor to the local business ecosystem. The Chamber of Commerce can be the catalyst that propels your venture toward sustained success and community impact.

CHAPTER 19
Social Media Presence

Social Media Presence for Your Food Truck Business

In the digital age, a strong social media presence is a non-negotiable component of any successful business, and food trucks are no exception. Social media platforms not only act as a direct line of communication with your customers but also serve as powerful marketing tools. Here's why establishing and maintaining a robust social media presence is vital for your food truck venture:

1. Visibility and Brand Awareness:

- **Platform Selection:** Identify and prioritize the social media platforms that resonate most with your target audience. Platforms like Instagram, Facebook, Twitter, and TikTok are popular choices for food-related businesses.

- **Consistent Branding:** Maintain a consistent brand identity across all platforms. This includes using the same logo, color scheme, and tone of voice. This coherence helps in building brand recognition.

2. Customer Engagement:

- **Regular Updates:** Keep your audience engaged with regular updates. Share behind-the-scenes glimpses of your food truck, introduce new menu items,

- and showcase the team. This creates a personal connection with your customers.

- **Interactive Content:** Encourage engagement through polls, contests, and questions. Prompt your audience to share their experiences, favorite dishes, or suggestions. This two-way interaction fosters a sense of community.

3. Professional Visuals:

- **High-Quality Imagery:** Invest in high-quality, professional photos of your food items. Visual appeal is a significant factor in the food industry, and enticing images can attract customers.

- **Consistent Aesthetic:** Maintain a consistent visual aesthetic on your profile. This helps create a cohesive and visually appealing feed.

4. Marketing and Promotion:

- **Special Offers:** Leverage social media to promote special offers, discounts, or limited-time menu items. This can create a sense of urgency and drive customer traffic.

- **Collaborations:** Explore collaborations with local influencers, food bloggers, or other businesses. These partnerships can expand your reach and introduce your food truck to new audiences.

5. Customer Reviews and Feedback:

- **Monitor Reviews:** Keep a close eye on reviews and comments. Respond promptly and professionally to both positive and negative feedback. This demonstrates your commitment to customer satisfaction.

6. Hiring a Social Media Manager:

- **Professional Content:** Consider hiring a local social media manager. They can ensure your social media accounts are consistently updated with professional content, including high-quality photos and engaging captions.

- **Strategic Posting:** A social media manager can develop and execute a content calendar, ensuring regular and strategic posting. This consistency is key to maintaining an active and relevant online presence.

Remember, a well-managed social media presence not only attracts customers but also builds a community around your brand. It's a dynamic tool to showcase the personality of your food truck business and keep your audience excited about what you have to offer.

CHAPTER 20
Seasonal Considerations

Seasonal Considerations for Your Food Truck Business

Running a food truck comes with the unique challenge of adapting to seasonal changes, which can significantly impact your business. Here's an exploration of how seasonal variations can affect your food truck and strategies for effectively navigating these changes:

1. Menu Adaptation:

- **Seasonal Ingredients:** Tailor your menu to incorporate seasonal ingredients. This not only ensures freshness but also aligns with the preferences of customers during specific times of the year.

- **Specialty Items:** Introduce seasonal or holiday-themed specialty items. This adds variety to your menu and can create a sense of excitement among customers.

2. Marketing Strategies:

- **Promote Seasonal Offerings:** Use your social media platforms and other marketing channels to highlight seasonal offerings. Consider running promotions or discounts for seasonal items to attract customers.

- **Engage with Seasonal Events:** Participate in or organize events that are popular during specific seasons. This could include festivals, fairs, or community gatherings. Tailor your marketing to align with these events.

3. Operational Flexibility:

- **Adjust Operating Hours:** Depending on the season, consider adjusting your operating hours to match the patterns of customer traffic. Longer hours during peak seasons and shorter hours during slower periods can optimize your business.

- **Mobile vs. Stationary:** Evaluate whether it makes sense to be mobile or stationary during certain seasons. For example, being stationary in a popular location during the winter may attract more foot traffic.

4. Seasonal Decor and Ambiance:

- **Create a Seasonal Atmosphere:** Enhance the visual appeal of your food truck by incorporating seasonal decor. This creates a welcoming atmosphere and can attract customers in the festive spirit.

- **Themed Events:** Consider organizing themed events based on seasons. This not only adds a unique touch to your business but also encourages customer engagement.

5. Weather-Related Considerations:

- **Weather-Appropriate Offerings:** Adjust your menu based on weather conditions. For example, offer refreshing items during hot summers and hearty, warm dishes during colder months.

- **Weather-Resistant Setup:** Ensure that your food truck is equipped to handle various weather conditions. This includes having proper coverings, heaters, or cooling systems as needed.

6. Community Engagement:

- **Seasonal Partnerships:** Collaborate with local businesses or vendors for seasonal partnerships. This could involve joint promotions or participating in community events together.

- **Seasonal Loyalty Programs:** Introduce seasonal loyalty programs to encourage repeat business during specific times of the year.

7. Inventory Management:

- **Seasonal Inventory Planning:** Plan your inventory based on seasonal demand. Avoid overstocking items that may have lower demand during certain seasons.

- **Limited-Time Offers:** Create a sense of urgency by introducing limited-time offers for seasonal items. This can drive sales and create anticipation among customers.

8. Data Analysis:

- **Track Seasonal Trends:** Use data analytics to track seasonal trends in your sales. This information can guide future business decisions and help you anticipate and prepare for seasonal fluctuations.

Adapting to seasonal changes requires a combination of creativity, flexibility, and strategic planning. By aligning your menu, marketing efforts, and operations with seasonal trends, you can optimize your food truck business for success throughout the year.

CHAPTER 21
Collaborations and Partnerships

Collaborations and Partnerships: Fostering a Food Truck Family

In the vibrant world of food trucks, building a sense of community and camaraderie among fellow vendors can significantly enhance the success of your venture. Here's an exploration of the potential benefits and effective approaches to collaborations and partnerships, emphasizing the importance of creating a food truck family:

1. Collective Customer Reach:

- **Unified Promotions:** Partner with other food trucks for unified promotions. Coordinated efforts, such as joint discounts or thematic events, create a more significant impact and attract a broader customer base.

- **Food Truck Rallies:** Organize food truck rallies where multiple vendors come together. This not only draws larger crowds but also provides customers with diverse culinary options, turning the event into a community celebration.

2. Collaborative Events and Experiences:

- **Joint Culinary Experiences:** Collaborate with fellow food trucks to offer joint culinary experiences. This could involve creating shared menus or organizing events where customers can enjoy a variety of dishes from different trucks.

- **Food Truck Festivals:** Participate in food truck festivals as a group. Showcase the diversity of your offerings collectively, turning the festival into a food exploration adventure for attendees.

3. Supportive Network:

- **Information Sharing:** Establish a supportive network where food truck owners share information and insights. This could include tips on popular locations, event opportunities, or challenges encountered and overcome.

- **Emergency Assistance:** Create a system for emergency assistance among food trucks. For example, if one truck faces technical issues, others can step in to help, ensuring a seamless experience for customers.

4. Shared Resources for Efficiency:

- **Resource Pooling:** Collaborate on resource-sharing initiatives. This might involve jointly purchasing supplies, sharing equipment, or coordinating maintenance efforts to maximize efficiency.

- **Combined Marketing Efforts:** Pool resources for marketing campaigns. By combining efforts, you can reach a larger audience and promote the food truck community as a whole.

5. Collective Community Engagement:

- **Group Sponsorships:** Collaborate on sponsoring local initiatives as a group of food trucks. This showcases a collective commitment to the community and strengthens the impact of your involvement.

- **Community Events Participation:** Engage in community events together. This not only amplifies your presence but also fosters a sense of unity and shared purpose within the local food truck community.

6. Variety and Diversity in Menus:

- **Menu Diversity Collaboration:** Partner with other food trucks to create diverse menu options. Encourage customers to explore different culinary experiences within the food truck family, promoting a sense of inclusivity.

- **Featured Food Truck Days:** Designate specific days for featuring each food truck within the group. This rotation keeps the offerings fresh and exciting for regular customers.

7. Collective Loyalty Programs:

- **Joint Loyalty Initiatives:** Develop joint loyalty programs encompassing all participating food trucks. Customers can earn and redeem rewards across the entire food truck family, encouraging repeat business and loyalty.

8. Social Media Collaboration:

- **Collaborative Social Media Campaigns:** Coordinate social media campaigns with other food trucks. Share each other's posts, collaborate on content creation, and celebrate the diversity of the food truck community on digital platforms.

9. Knowledge and Skill Exchange:

- **Skill-Building Workshops:** Organize workshops within the food truck family for skill exchange. This can involve sharing culinary techniques, business insights, or creative ideas to uplift the entire community.

10. Unified Presence at Events:

- **Coordinated Event Presence:** Coordinate attendance at events to ensure a unified presence. This not only enhances the collective impact but also showcases the diversity and richness of the local food truck scene.

In embracing a collaborative mindset and viewing fellow food trucks as allies rather than competitors, you contribute to the growth and vibrancy of a food truck family. By working together, sharing experiences, and celebrating each other's successes, you foster a supportive community that benefits everyone involved, from vendors to customers alike.

CHAPTER 22
Entrepreneurship Unleashed

Culinary Entrepreneurship Unleashed

Congratulations on reaching the final chapter of "Rolling Success: A Comprehensive Guide to Launching Your Food Truck Business." As you reflect on the journey we've embarked upon, let's distill the essence of our culinary entrepreneurship guide and explore the key takeaways that will serve as your compass in navigating the exciting world of food trucks.

1. From Vision to Reality: Your Culinary Adventure Begins

- Recall the spark that ignited your passion for the food truck dream. Whether it was a love for crafting delectable dishes or a desire for culinary freedom, your journey began with a vision. Embrace the reality you've created, transforming aspirations into a tangible food truck venture.

2. Foundations of Success: Planning and Preparation

- Lay the groundwork for triumph with meticulous planning. Understand the nuances of crafting a business plan, securing necessary permits, and envisioning your brand. Success is built on a foundation of preparation, and your thorough groundwork ensures resilience in the face of challenges.

3. The Heart of Your Business: Culinary Craftsmanship

- Your food truck is not merely a vehicle; it's a culinary stage. Hone your craft, curate a menu that tantalizes taste buds, and infuse your unique flavor into every dish. Elevate your offerings, making each meal a memorable experience for your customers.

4. Navigating the Streets: Strategic Locations and Events

- The journey of a food truck involves navigating diverse terrains. Discover prime locations, engage in bustling events, and become a staple in your community. Adaptability and strategic placement amplify your visibility, making your food truck a sought-after destination.

5. Collaborative Excellence: Building a Food Truck Family

- Elevate your business by embracing collaboration over competition. Forming alliances with fellow food trucks creates a supportive ecosystem. Share insights, pool resources, and celebrate successes together. A united food truck family strengthens the entire community.

6. Financial Mastery: Beyond Profits to Sustainable Growth

- Delve into the financial intricacies of your food truck venture. From tax management to profit allocation, cultivate financial discipline. Set up separate accounts, pay taxes regularly, and earmark funds for both profit and growth. Financial mastery propels your journey towards sustainable expansion.

7. Beyond the Truck: Marketing, Social Media, and Community Engagement

- Extend your influence beyond the confines of your truck. Craft a compelling brand narrative, harness the power of social media, and actively engage with your community. Building a brand transcends the physical space of your truck, creating lasting connections with customers.

8. Ensuring Compliance: Safety, Health, and Employee Management

- Prioritize safety, health, and compliance. Adhere to regulations, maintain impeccable hygiene, and, if applicable, manage your team effectively. Upholding standards ensures the longevity of your venture and fosters trust among both customers and stakeholders.

9. Adapting to Seasons: Navigating Changes and Staying Relevant

- Seasons change, and so does the culinary landscape. Adapt your menu, marketing strategies, and operational approach based on seasonal trends. Staying relevant requires a dynamic mindset, enabling your food truck to thrive in every season.

10. The Culinary Odyssey Continues: A Future of Possibilities

- As we conclude this guide, remember that your culinary odyssey is an ever-evolving journey. Seize opportunities, embrace challenges, and savor the richness of your experiences. It's food truck is not just a business; it's a canvas for your culinary artistry, continually painting a future filled with possibilities.

It will be extremely hard work! But may your food truck journey be seasoned with triumphs, creativity, and a dash of entrepreneurial spirit. Here's to the thriving success of your culinary endeavors!

Happy Rolling!

Success Navigator

Congratulations on your journey to launch a successful food truck business! Use this comprehensive checklist to ensure you've covered all crucial aspects discussed in "All the Crap Nobody Told Me," A Practical Guide to Starting Your Food Truck Business!

1. Vision and Planning:

o Crafted a compelling vision for your food truck venture.

o Developed a detailed business plan, outlining your goals, target audience, and financial projections.

2. Legalities and Permits:

o Checked local requirements for licenses, permits, and inspections.

o Obtained necessary licenses and permits, including health department approval.

o Scheduled and passed inspections for your food truck.

3. Culinary Craftsmanship:

o Curated a diverse and appealing menu that showcases your culinary expertise.

o Ensured the availability of high-quality ingredients and perfected your signature dishes.

4. Strategic Locations and Events:

o Explored and secured prime locations for daily operations.

o Researched and participated in local events, festivals, and markets.

o Established relationships with property owners for potential locations.

5. Collaborative Excellence:

o Connected with other food truck owners and formed collaborative partnerships.

o   Actively participated in local food truck communities and events.

6. Financial Mastery:

o   Set up separate bank accounts for taxes, profits, and growth.

o   Implemented a system for regular tax payments, either daily or weekly.

o   Calculated and allocated profits for business growth.

7. Marketing and Social Media Presence:

o   Crafted a compelling brand narrative.

o   Established and maintained a robust social media presence.

o   Engaged with the community through online platforms.

8. Ensuring Compliance:

o   Maintained high standards of safety and cleanliness.

o   Managed employees effectively, if applicable.

o   Kept detailed records of health and safety compliance.

9. Adapting to Seasons:

o   Developed strategies for adapting the menu and marketing based on seasonal changes.

o   Stayed informed about upcoming seasonal trends in the food industry.

10. Continuous Improvement:

o   Implemented systems for customer feedback and actively sought reviews.

o   Regularly reviewed and updated your business plan.

o   Evaluated the success of partnerships and collaborations.

Conclusion:

o   Reviewed the entire "Rolling Success" guide to ensure no steps were overlooked.

o   Celebrated the exciting journey ahead as you launch your food truck business!

Best of luck on your culinary adventure!

Thank you for embarking on this food truck journey with "All the Crap Nobody Told Me." Your success matters to us, and we're here to support you every step of the way. If you have any questions, or concerns, or simply want to share your thoughts on how the book has impacted you, please feel free to reach out. We welcome your feedback!

Contact Information:

- Email: admin@buluj.com

- Website: www.road-tisserie.com

- Social Media:

- *Facebook: @road-tisserie*
- *Instagram: @road-tisserie*
- *TikTok: @roadtisserie*

Explore Our Spice Collection:

Elevate your culinary creations with our signature spice blends, available online or at select stores. Visit our website to discover more!

Your success is our delight, and we look forward to hearing about your thriving food truck venture. Happy rolling!

www.ingramcontent.com/pod-product-compliance
Lightning Source LLC
Chambersburg PA
CBHW082245310526
45795CB00015B/2996